Intro

The Black Lives Matter organization is everywhere today, and millions of people, including churches, organizations, and political powers are marching alongside them, but do they really know for what and with whom they are actually marching? I am an African American man who, instead of jumping on the bandwagon, chooses to research the coachman driving the carriage.

I will present undisputable proof that exposes this organization and its founders for who they really are. While they claim to advocate for black lives, their actual preference lies in gay and transgender rights. Their political movement is also a deeply spiritual movement that involves heavy witchcraft, and I will direct you to actual footage of these ceremonies performed by the movement's founders. They are trained Marxists as well, seeking to conform their followers to the same political agenda. As they pursue overthrowing a heteronormative society, this movement ultimately aims to destroy the church.

In directing you to this compilation of evidence, my hope is to educate churches and Americans at large as to the real agenda at the heart of this organization. This is urgently needed, now more than ever, as this movement is rapidly growing in cities and towns across our country, in corporate boardrooms and children's classrooms, in political offices and all levels of government, among members of churches everywhere, and in the very fabric of our society and culture.

Chapter 1
Hidden Gay & Transgender Agenda

Black Lives Matter Global Network Foundation, the organization's official name, purports to be a non-profit concerned with the equality of black people, particularly as it pertains to police brutality. I set out to understand exactly what they represented by directly reading their own self-description on their website. Typically, most foundations have a mission statement that asserts their primary intentions and goals. *(updated note: BLM has just changed its Mission Statement of 7 years to a generic one, because people were already exposing them), but look up the old one.*

Taken at face value, one can already observe a fundamental veering from violence against the black community. They claim, "We are guided by the fact that all Black lives matter, regardless of actual or perceived sexual identity, gender identity, gender expression. . . ."[1] Why, in the context of discussing race, do they focus on sexual identity, gender identity, and gender expression? What does the identity of one's gender or sexual preference have to do with black lives or police brutality? It doesn't. Such a problematic

---

[1] "What We Believe," *Black Lives Matter*, https://blacklivesmatter.com/what-we-believe/.

finding compelled me to dive deeper into their "What We Believe" page.

They claim, "We make space for transgender brothers and sisters to participate and lead."[2] Again, the spotlight is on non-black identity, even though they label their movement Black Lives Matter (BLM). But having an exclusive, stand-alone sentence in their list of beliefs to underscore the importance of transgenderism? It's strange considering that every protest thus far has been for a black man who died by the hands of police, such as Michael Brown and George Floyd.

More research was necessary to figure out the reason for such jarring content on their website, so any further explanation must lie with the founders themselves. The organization was established by three women: Alicia Garza, Patrisse Cullors, and Opal Tometi.[3] Garza, the primary founder, is an openly gay, black woman who is married to Malachi Garza, a transgender man. This could certainly account for the heavy focus on sexual identity over race. Cullors is also openly queer (i.e. sexual and gender minorities who are not heterosexual and cisgender).

As I continued to peruse their mission statement, what I read next chilled me to the bone: "We are self-reflexive and

---

[2] "What We Believe," *Black Lives Matter*.
[3] "Black Lives Matter," *Wikipedia,* accessed August 12, 2020, https://en.wikipedia.org/wiki/Black_Lives_Matter.

do the work required to dismantle cisgender privilege and uplift Black trans folk, especially Black trans women."[4] Notice how they refrain from saying "black folk" in general, but black *"trans"* folk, and black *"trans"* women. This excludes most of the group it has publicly been claiming to represent! If this is their mission statement—their cause, their goal—it has nothing to do with uplifting the black community as a whole, not even as it pertains to police brutality.

As stated, they aim to "dismantle cisgender privilege." I had never even heard of such a word. "Cisgender" is a recent term coined by progressives to denote "a person whose gender identity corresponds with the sex the person had or was identified as having at birth."[5] It's simply a traditional man or woman, but one weapon in their arsenal is language. Through introducing new terms into society and culture at large, they hope to overthrow what is considered normal and normalize the abnormal. So, BLM is attempting to tear down and reverse, or "dismantle," the "privileges" within society that a traditional person receives.

Their goal, however, is not equal rights, but stripping the traditional man and woman of theirs. To take away others' rights certainly seems to go *against* what they claim they are protesting. Again, what does this have to do with black

---

[4] "What We Believe," *Black Lives Matter*.
[5] Merriam-Webster.com Dictionary, s.v. "cisgender," accessed August 12, 2020, https://www.merriam-webster.com/dictionary/cisgender.

equality or police brutality? I am a black man, and my life matters, so why would they be marching to take away my beliefs and rights? Do *all* black lives truly matter to them?

Continuing in their statement of beliefs, BLM affirms, "We disrupt the Western-prescribed nuclear family structure requirement by supporting each other as extended families and 'villages' that collectively care for one another."[6] Such a loaded assertion warrants breaking down. First, what is the "Western-prescribed nuclear family?" The structure consists of two parents living with their children, also known as an immediate family.[7] Note that the founders did not say they wanted equal rights for their atypical family structures, but to disrupt the typical. "Disrupt" means to rupture, destroy, or break to pieces. Their self-confessed goal is to destroy the traditional family structure that Americans certainly have the right to maintain. Once again, any attempt to claim equal rights within this movement fall flat, since they seek to abolish the right to a traditional home.

DeRay Mckesson, one of the top leaders of the BLM movement, ran for Baltimore mayor in 2016.[8] He has underscored that "advocacy for the LGBTQ community [is]

---

[6] "What We Believe," *Black Lives Matter*.
[7] "Nuclear Family," *Wikipedia,* accessed August 12, 2020, https://en.wikipedia.org/wiki/Nuclear_family.
[8] "The Leading Global Thinkers of 2015," Advocates, *Foreign Policy*, https://2015globalthinkers.foreignpolicy.com/#!advocates/list.

a primary mission for the movement."[9] There are numerous articles with statements from the founders and the BLM board of directors that confirm the paramount mission is about pushing the LGBTQ+ agenda. There is even an article, entitled "From the start, Black Lives Matter has been about LGBTQ lives," that left-leaning ABC News published, admitting the actual roots of the movement.[10] Several other stories will be listed at the end of this book that also include declarations that if a person is pro-black, he or she *has* to be pro-LGBTQ. When has being a proponent of racial equality been inextricably tied to endorsing another unrelated cause?

The LGBTQ+ advocacy has been so fundamental to their real mission that it has become the underlying, covert impetus for marches: "When we gather, we do so with the intention of freeing ourselves from the tight grip of heteronormative thinking."[11] So what is "heteronormative thinking?" It relates to a worldview that promotes heterosexuality as the normal or preferred sexual

---

[9] Allana Haynes, "The Great Divide: Why The Church Isn't Connecting With #BLM," *Religion Unplugged,* May 29, 2020, https://religionunplugged.com/news/2017/7/25/the-church-and-black-lives-matter.

[10] Sony Salzman, "From the start, Black Lives Matter has been about LGBTQ live," *Religion Unplugged,* June 21, 2020, https://religionunplugged.com/news/2017/7/25/the-church-and-black-lives-matter.

[11] "What We Believe," *Black Lives Matter.*

orientation.[12] Each rally, regardless of signs held for George Floyd or Trevon Martin, was essentially a march for liberating themselves from the confines of normal, sexual orientation.

As early as 2015, LGBTQ+ organizations have been standing alongside the BLM movement in solidarity.[13] Many news stories have reported on the close ties between BLM and this community from the organization's inception, including financial support; these groups have even admitted their combining of resources in hopes of making further progress. While it appears that blacks are merely being used as pawns for this radical agenda, I will unfold how even the LGBTQ+ community is being used by this organization for even deeper ulterior motives.

---

[12] Merriam-Webster.com Dictionary, s.v. "heteronormative," accessed August 12, 2020, https://www.merriam-webster.com/dictionary/heteronormative.

[13] Jennifer Houston, "LGBTQ Organizations Stand in Solidarity with Black Lives Matter," *Neighborhood Funders Group,* December 3, 2015, https://www.nfg.org/news/lgbtq-organizations-stand-solidarity-black-lives-matter.

Chapter 2
Hidden Witchcraft Agenda

Not only does the Black Lives Matter movement have an ulterior agenda for gay and transgender rights, they are also alarmingly tied to witchcraft. Though they certainly present themselves as a secular political activist group, it is highly demonic. Through this chapter I will prove to you that co-founder of BLM Patrisse Cullors not only performs witchcraft, she is a high priestess, infusing witchcraft and voodoo in the movement, co-authoring books acknowledging it, and even performing witchcraft and séances publicly. She has stated in dozens of interviews that BLM is a **spiritual movement**, and that **it has always been so**[14] (emphasis added). That's a remarkably profound statement. Cullors states that chanting victims' names is "'literally almost resurrecting a spirit so they can work through us to get the work that we need to get done.'"[15] So, understanding that this is not a secular organization, what does she mean by "spiritual?" To what "spirits" is she referring?

---

[14] Lawrence Burnley, "The Movement for Black Lives Has Always Been Spiritual," *Yes! Magazine,* June 19, 2020, https://www.yesmagazine.org/opinion/2020/06/19/black-lives-movement-spiritual/.

[15] Alejandra Molina, "Black Lives Matter is 'a spiritual movement,' says co-founder Patrisse Cullors," *Religion News Service*, June 15, 2020, https://religionnews.com/2020/06/15/why-black-lives-matter-is-a-spiritual-movement-says-blm-co-founder-patrisse-cullors/.

Cullors grew up as a Jehovah's Witness, but left the tradition at an early age. In a 2015 interview, she shared:

> "By 12, 13, I knew that this was not the place for me, but I felt very connected to spirit. So the question became, what is the place for me?" she said. She turned to her great-grandmother, who is from the Choctaw and Blackfoot tribes, and talked to her about her great-grandfather, a medicine man. Her interest in indigenous spirituality led to Ifà.[16]

Ifà is a western African religion that practices **voodoo, black magic**, and divination that is associated with ancestor worship.[17] Not only does she believe in Ifà, she is a teacher of witchcraft

(Picture of Ifà worship in Africa)

---

[16] Heba H Farrag, "The Role of the Spirit in the #blacklivesmatter Movement: A Conversation with Activist and Artist Patrisse Cullors," *Religion Dispatches*, June 24, 2015, https://religiondispatches.org/the-role-of-spirit-in-the-blacklivesmatter-movement-a-conversation-with-activist-and-artist-patrisse-cullors/.
[17] "Ifà," *Wikipedia*, accessed August 12, 2020, https://en.wikipedia.org/wiki/If%C3%A1.

and holds a very high position of authority in it. In *Farming While Black*, author Leah Penniman acknowledges Cullors for teaching her to "hear [her] ancestors and how to divine."[18] She addresses her as "Ìyánífá," which is a title role within this black magic, satanic religion.[19] The word means "mother of divination or wisdom," and designates a priestess.[20] This leadership position divines and teaches voodoo to others, so she plays no minor role in this false religion.[21] When she says it's a spiritual movement, then, these are the spirits to which she is referring. In fact, Cullors brings this experience to the BLM rallies, where they "use a lot of [the] indigenous practices."[22] She is clearly a sincere believer and advocate for African witchcraft: "For Patrisse Cullors, spirituality saves souls."[23] It's shocking how little is reported of this in the broad coverage of the BLM movement in the mainstream news—to the point that such a claim might seem baseless, but there is

---

[18] Leah Penniman, *Farming While Black: Soul Fire Farm's Practical Guide to Liberation on the Land* (White River Junction, VT: Chelsea Green Publishing, 2018), 70.
[19] "Iyalawo," *Wikipedia,* accessed August 12, 2020, https://en.wikipedia.org/wiki/Iyalawo.
[20] "Iyanifa, Women of Wisdom," *Iyanifa,* http://www.iyanifa.org/home.html.
[21] "Ifà Religion: Iyanifa, Mother of Wisdom," https://ifa-odu.com/iyanifa-ifa-priestess/.
[22] Tippett, Krista. Interview with Patrissee Cullors and Bob Ross. "On Being with Krista Tippett: Patrisse Cullors + Bob Ross, The Spiritual Work of Black Lives Matter." *National Public Radio*, February 18, 2016, https://onbeing.org/programs/patrisse-cullors-and-robert-ross-the-spiritual-work-of-black-lives-matter-may2017/.
[23] Farrag, "Role of Spirit."

ample evidence upon deeper digging, including her own admission.

She has self-identified as an Ifà practitioner.[24] In *When They Call You a Terrorist: A Black Lives Matter Memoir*, Cullors shares how her life is dedicated to Olodumare, a god within the pagan religion; her personal life, relationships, and the movement all revolve around it.[25] According to the Orisha manual within the religion, Ifà is a gateway spirit to access Olodumare. The religion maintains spiritual possession allows this god to move and respond to human concerns through divination, possession, sacrifice and more.[26]

(Book cover for Ifà Religion)

---

[24] Vincent Lloyd, et al, "Religion, secularism, and Black Lives Matter," *The Immanent Frame, Social Science Research Council*, September 22, 2016, https://tif.ssrc.org/2016/09/22/religion-secularism-and-black-lives-matter/.
[25] Patrisse Khan-Cullors and Asha Bandele, *When They Call You a Terrorist: A Black Lives Matter Memoir* (New York: St. Martin's Publishing Group, 2018).
[26] "Yoruba People," *Wikipedia*, accessed on August 12, 2020, https://en.wikipedia.org/wiki/Yoruba_people#Religion_and_mythology.

Considering all of the evidence, witchcraft undoubtedly plays a role in the movement. Its incorporation is admittedly integrated into all levels of the movement, including rallies in which unsuspecting marchers are participating. Aside from their declared fight for racial justice, BLM aims to liberate the mind and the spirit. It encourages "healing justice," which employs alternative medicine and psychotherapy on its subjects, so that people can heal from trauma. Cullors purposely uses witchcraft in this movement.

In a separate article for Georgetown University, writer Hebah Farrag reports, "The movement infuses a syncretic blend of African and indigenous cultures' spiritual practices and beliefs, embracing ancestor worship; Ifà-based ritual such as chanting, dancing, and summoning deities.[27] Cullors openly shares how she leads meditations with participants. Farrag astutely observes: "Some see BLM as secularizing the new civil rights movement. Instead, BLM's marginalization of patriarchal and hierarchical modalities of religion informs its members' reinterpretation and expression of faith, political expression, radical organizing, and community-building."[28]

It is patently clear that this movement was created and primarily run based on the Ifà religion, not secularism—and

---

[27] Hebah Farrag, "The Fight for Black Lives is a Spiritual Movement," *Berkely Center for Religion, Peace, and World Affairs, Georgetown University*, June 9, 2020, https://berkleycenter.georgetown.edu/responses/the-fight-for-black-lives-is-a-spiritual-movement.
[28] Ibid.

that religion is a far cry from biblical Christianity. The movement is inextricably tied to the religious component. In fact, **Cullors even goes beyond that, saying the movement cannot be successful without witchcraft,** admitting that the strong elements of witchcraft and false gods are essential as political engagement alone will not accomplish the goals:

> "Participants engaged in these spiritual practices know that social transformation involves politics and policy, but they believe that transformative work is ***ultimately*** a spiritual effort that requires a shift in consciousness. Although Black Lives Matter is predominantly a political and ideological movement, its co-founder Patrisse Cullors explains that political engagement alone will not accomplish the transformative work that needs to occur."[29]

Even though mainstream society believes the BLM organization is merely a political movement marching against police brutality, the heart of the work is fundamentally a spiritual undertaking that necessitates indoctrination to engender an alteration in consciousness. In other words, they seek to subconsciously shift spiritual views. Christians must

---

[29] Elise M. Edwards, "'Let's Imagine Something Different': Spiritual Principles in Contemporary African American Justice Movements and Their Implications for the Built Environment." *Religions* 8, 12, 2017: https://www.mdpi.com/2077-1444/8/12/256/htm.

understand that the movement's goals are comprehensively inspired by satanic witchcraft, dressed up in secular, psychobabble garb. Though some readers may be thinking, *I don't see any of this at the events,* it is there, whether you know it or not.

The same article documents how "participants in the movement incorporate spiritual practices into traditional forms of protest and civic engagement," even engaging in rituals such as burning incense and constructing altars.[30] Satanists and witches online have been rallying support across their online community, calling for demonic spells of protection for protestors during the marches, along with hexes on the police:

> Comprised mostly of teens and young women who look to the dark arts for "empowerment," these witches are following the lead of a TikTok user named venxm.exe who filmed herself casting a protection spell for protestors. Within five days, the tag #witchesforblm had 10 million views, and now serves as a meeting place for practicing witches who want to get involved in the politics of the day.[31]

---

[30] Edwards, "'Let's Imagine Something Different.'"
[31] Susan Brinckmann, "Witchcraft Invades the BLM Movement," *Women of Grace*, June 16, 2020, https://www.womenofgrace.com/blog/?p=72316.

Postings suggest specific hexes aimed at bringing misfortune to police officers who interfere with the protests. The American Society for the Defense of Tradition, Family and Property's John Horvat II laments, "'A generation that has grown up without organized religions which it deemed "outdated" is now filling the void with hopelessly ancient pagan deities.'"[32] He continues, warning, "'This is why the involvement of witches in the protests is so troubling to those Christians who understand the full implications of dark magic.'"[33] He chronicles:

> [W]itches' covens are actively engaged in hexing police, whom they accuse of brutality. They especially target those who are risking their lives to stop the riots. The witches also cast spells asking for protection for protestors that confront the police. Witch activists used their dark arts as cutting-edge weapons for those who want to engage in a more spiritual class warfare. . . . The postings often include videos of witches casting spells or even acting out what they believe will happen to the police they target. The hexing can get very personal as the witches teach others to write down the names of individual police officers on papers, which are then burned with black candles. The hexes aim to bring

---

[32] Brinckmann, "Witchcraft."
[33] Ibid.

misfortune to the officers already at risk while defending the city from disorder.34

With Cullors at the helm, this occult activism is demonstrably not just a peripheral sideshow of the movement as mainstream news attempts to portray, but a palpable representation of the real spiritual underpinnings of the entire organization. Cullors has even openly orchestrated witchcraft publicly in demonstrations, such as her recent "Prayer to the Iyami" performance.35 **This** was an open prayer in public that she performed with media, reporters, and hundreds of spectators. It looked innocent, but she truncated the title of the prayer—the full name is Iyami Aje.

(Photograph of Cullors' Performance)

---

34 John Horvat II, "Witches and Satanists have teamed up with leftists to destroy America," *Lifesite News*, June 16, 2020, https://www.lifesitenews.com/opinion/witches-and-satanists-have-teamed-up-with-leftists-to-destroy-america.

35 Gabriella Angeleti, "Watch Patrisse Cullors' 'Prayer to the Iyami' Performance," *The Art Newspaper*, June 4, 2020, https://www.theartnewspaper.com/video/patrisse-cullors-prayer-to-the-iyami.

Iyami Aje is a Yoruba term for a powerful witch: "aje" "signifies the biological and spiritual power of African women that has myriad potential, including but not limited to, powers of elemental, biological and artistic creation; healing; destruction; spiritual and physical development and fortification; and political organization and empowerment."[36] The linguistic structure of "Iyami" renders a maternal connotation that translates as "'the super-powerful ones.'"[37] Praying to this mother witch provides a gateway to the Ifà Olodumare god. Within the Ifà religion, public worship is purposed to cause an altered state of consciousness,[38] which uncannily resembles Cullors prior remarks that BLM's goals are "ultimately a spiritual effort that requires a shift in consciousness."[39] It's clear she knows exactly what she's doing, even while naïve Americans, corporations, and organizations latch on to the BLM crusade.

Cullors and others direct those within the movement to "join traditional forms of social protest and policy development with rituals and spiritual practices, drawing upon spiritual resources as a source of transformation and empowerment."[40] Many events echo the doctrines of

---

[36] "Iyami Aje," *Wikipedia,* accessed August 12, 2020, https://en.wikipedia.org/wiki/Iyami_Aje.
[37] "Iyami Aje," *Wikipedia.*
[38] "Orisha Worshipers," *Federal Bureau of Prisons,* https://www.bop.gov/foia/docs/orishamanual.pdf.
[39] Edwards, "'Let's Imagine Something Different.'"
[40] Ibid.

liberation theology, an unorthodox offshoot religion to which co-founder Alicia Garza subscribes; others promote and teach spiritual well-being, slowly introducing the dark arts in the tenets of Ifà to unknowing supporters.[41] Final co-founder Opal Tometi has the same background.

Ironically, while this aspect of the BLM movement is the most concerning, it is the most underreported. Thus, educating the public on these matters is absolutely essential. Understanding that a founder of this organization not only practices witchcraft, but is a high-ranking priestess in a satanic religion, that she created the movement to infuse witchcraft and obtain results unachievable otherwise, and that she and other leaders orchestrated public performances of voodoo is critical to preventing the growth of Black Lives Matter.

---

[41] Farrag, "Role of Spirit."

Chapter 3
Hidden Marxist Agenda

Admittedly not a fan of politics in general, I sought to educate myself on Marxism. The term has been thrown around in American political circles recently, and so a precise understanding of the ideology is key. In its truest form, Marxism is a "method of socioeconomic analysis that uses a materialist interpretation of historical development, better known as historical materialism, to understand class relations and social conflict as well as a dialectical perspective to view social transformation."[42] In short, Marxists are typically political communists who interpret "social transformation" as overthrowing the government and anyone else who opposes them. Stemming from the works of Karl Marx and Friedrich Engels, both 19th-century German philosophers, these theories were primarily economic in nature, although they have been applied in many areas since.

The most notable example is communism, a political form of Marxist economic theory. Aside from espousing beliefs fundamentally antithetical to American principles of liberty, this ideology led to 94 million deaths in the 20th

---

[42] "Marxism," *Wikipedia,* accessed on August 12, 2020, https://en.wikipedia.org/wiki/Marxism.

century; fascism netted a paltry 28 million, by comparison, though garnering more attention in history books.[43] Needless to say, most Americans are highly intolerant of this deadly political system, as the Cold War has testified.

Marxism considers itself to be the "embodiment of scientific socialism," and a cultural application of this theory is rapidly gaining steam in America.[44] Marxism dictates that society is broken into two groups: the oppressors and the oppressed. Cultural Marxists believe the oppressed group has the right to overthrow this cultural hegemony by overturning the current system and implementing their own. Popular among the political left, this idea has combined with "critical theory" to include "intersectionality," a way of measuring one's level of oppression on this spectrum.[45] Gender, religion, sexual orientation, nationality, and more, all play a role in determining the degree of subjugation.

The Black Lives Matter organization not only embraces this ideology, but was steeped in it. In fact, the Republican National Committee even capitalized off of co-founder

---

[43] John Walters, "Communism Killed 94M in 20th Century, Feels Need to Kill Again," *Reason*, March 13, 2013, https://reason.com/2013/03/13/communism-killed-94m-in-20th-century/.

[44] "Communism," *Wikipedia,* accessed on August 12, 2020, https://en.wikipedia.org/wiki/Communism.

[45] Neil Shenvi and Pat Sawyer, "The Incompatibility of Critical Theory and Christianity," *The Gospel Coalition*, May 15, 2019, https://www.thegospelcoalition.org/article/incompatibility-critical-theory-christianity/.

Patrisse Cullors' public statement that the BLM activists are "trained Marxists," in a recent campaign ad.[46]

Not only are they trained in how to topple the government, they have deep ties to terrorists and their organizations. Because BLM is not recognized by the IRS as a 501(c)3 non-profit organization, their funds are filtered through Thousand Currents, a non-profit financial sponsor for BLM.[47] Susan Rosenburg, who sits on the board of directors for this radical leftist organization, was a member of the terrorist organization May 19th Communist Organization, or M19CO, "a Marxist-Leninist group which openly advocates the overthrow of the U.S. Government through armed struggle and the use of violence," according to a contemporaneous FBI report.[48]

M19CO, formed by members of the radical Weather Underground, provided support to an offshoot of the Black Liberation Army, including armored truck robberies and

---

[46] Valerie Richardson, "'We are trained Marxists': Black Lives Matter co-founder featured in GOP ad," *The Washington Times,* June 25, 2020, https://www.washingtontimes.com/news/2020/jun/25/patrisse-cullors-black-lives-matter-co-founder-fea/.

[47] Jerry Dunleavy, "Black Lives Matter fundraising handled by group with convicted terrorist on its board," *Washington Examiner*, June 25, 2020, https://www.washingtonexaminer.com/news/black-lives-matter-fundraising-handled-by-group-with-convicted-terrorist-on-its-board.

[48] "FBI Analysis of Terrorist Incidents and Terrorist Related Activities in the United States 1984," https://www.ncjrs.gov/pdffiles1/Digitization/120257NCJRS.pdf.

later, government building bombings. Lingering on the FBI's Most Wanted List, Rosenberg was finally captured in 1984, while unloading hundreds of pounds of explosives and weapons.[49] After serving two decades in prison, President Bill Clinton commuted her sentence on his last day in office.[50] Since its inception, she has been aiding the organization. BLM co-founder Alicia Garza also claims domestic terrorist Assata Shakur as one of her primary inspirations; convicted of murdering a police officer in 1973, Shakur escaped from her life-sentence in prison and is currently on the FBI's Most Wanted List.[51] Once again, no major news coverage of any of this investigative reporting on an organization whose revenue stream skyrocketed with the killing of George Floyd; they raked in $33 million in less than a month following his death,[52] and are now worth over $1.6 billion.[53]

As a fundamentally Marxist organization, BLM's goal is to strategically take control of society through the political system and culture. They are a part of the Movement for Black

---

[49] Dunleavy, "Black Lives Matter."
[50] Andrew Kerr, "A Convicted Terrorist Sits On Board Of Charity Handling Black Lives Matter Fundraising," *Daily Caller*, June 27, 2020, https://dailycaller.com/2020/06/27/convicted-terrorist-black-lives-matter-thousand-currents/.
[51] Dunleavy, "Black Lives Matter."
[52] Ibid.
[53] William Michael Cunningham, "Black Lives Matter: Corporate America has Pledged at least $1.678 Billion So Far," *Black Enterprise*, June 10, 2020, https://www.blackenterprise.com/black-lives-matter-corporate-america-has-pledged-1-678-billion-so-far/.

Lives, a coalition of various black community interest groups, who released a policy handbook that serves as their platform.[54] They contend,

> We have created this platform to articulate and support the ambitions and work of Black people. We also seek to intervene in the current political climate and assert a clear vision, particularly for those who claim to be our allies, of the world we want them to help us create. We reject false solutions and believe we can achieve a complete transformation of the current systems, which place profit over people and make it impossible for many of us to breathe.[55]

Throughout this policy handbook, it becomes abundantly clear that they demand leadership void of all heterosexual, and especially heterosexual white men. Their radical feminism and contempt for men drip off the pages, to the extent of disavowing civil rights heroes because of their gender. Not only do Garza and Cullors intentionally reject the Christian framework that birthed much of the early civil rights movements, they actually oppose the civil rights framework itself. They believe some "have marginalized some of the

---

[54] "A Vision For Black Lives: Policy Demands for Black Power, Freedom, and Justice," *The Movement for Black Lives*, https://neweconomy.net/resources/vision-black-lives-policy-demands-black-power-freedom-and-justice.
[55] Ibid.

people they purport to fight for."⁵⁶ Garza explains, "'It goes beyond the narrow nationalism that can be prevalent within some Black communities, which merely call on Black people to love Black, live Black and buy Black, keeping straight cis Black men in the front of the movement.'"⁵⁷ Many in the black community who have donned BLM shirts, tweeted hashtags in support, or walked in marches may not realize this organization's purposeful condemnation of God, Martin Luther King, Jr., and the entire movement for civil rights.

The Movement for Black Lives demands political power in every aspect of society, necessitating a "remaking of the current U.S. political system in order to create a real democracy where Black people and all marginalized people can effectively exercise full political power."⁵⁸ The founders of BLM have constantly reiterated this idea in all of their interviews and statements. Ironically, they fail to see that such a system according to their professed beliefs would unequivocally be utterly undemocratic. After beholding the underbelly of the beast, protesting police brutality and advocating equal civil rights certainly seem a far cry from the real goals of BLM.

Can this be the first true successful takeover of society through Marxism in the United States? Organizations like this

---

⁵⁶ Edwards, "'Let's Imagine Something Different.'"
⁵⁷ Ibid.
⁵⁸ "A Vision For Black Lives," The Movement for Black Lives.

have long existed in this country, but never with such large-scale social acceptance as BLM receives now. This is cause for extreme concern. Worth almost $2 billion and even considered by some a political party,[59] the power they have amassed in this year alone is incredible, and it's displayed in their ability to silence all opposition. BLM wields the hammer of "cancel culture" to take out any dissidents. People have lost jobs for holding to views that don't fully align with BLM's ideology.[60] Athletes, journalists, and other public figures who don't unquestioningly support the movement are lambasted and ostracized on social media. Anyone opposing the street art and other BLM propaganda may be harassed or even physically assaulted.[61]

The state of the First Amendment in this country could be measured by any person publicly speaking out against the organization, even blacks—the very community they claim to represent! Protestors spew the most hate-filled speech imaginable, but rush to stifle any single voice of disagreement. For example, basketball star James Harden wore a mask supporting police, and protestors warned they would riot

---

[59] Morgan Phillips, "Could Black Lives Matter get on the ballot?" *Fox News,* June 25, 2020, https://www.foxnews.com/politics/black-lives-matter-ballot.

[60] John Daniel Davidson, "If You Don't Support Black Lives Matter, You're Fired," *The Federalist*, June 11, 2020, https://thefederalist.com/2020/06/11/if-you-dont-support-black-lives-matter-youre-fired/.

[61] Christina Zdanowicz and Artemis Moshtaghian, "Two people are charged with a hate crime for vandalizing a Black Lives Matter mural," *CNN*, July 7, 2020, https://www.cnn.com/2020/07/07/us/hate-crime-charges-black-lives-matter-mural-painted-over-trnd/index.html.

against the Houston Rockets' stadium, because an individual expressed a different opinion.[62]

Make no mistake. BLM has at least fifteen strategic goals:
1. Silence all opposition, especially public figures like news commentators, anchormen, and athletes who voice a different opinion, even if it results in lost jobs and death threats for the dissenters.
2. Abolish Judeo-Christian religion.[63]
3. Bring one or both political parties into subjection. The M4BL handbook states they seek to replace the current system.
4. Change policy by exploiting court rulings to weaken basic American institutions, such as court decisions that allow transgender athletes to unfairly compete (if LeBron James chose to identify as a woman, he could legally play in the WNBA, and any dissent would be deemed sex discrimination).
5. Control the public education system, such as introducing new curriculum that promotes abortion, same sex marriage, secular views, and an emphasis on

---

[62] Andrew Court, "'I thought it looked cool!' Houston Rockets star James Harden said he didn't intend to make a political statement after he sparked outrage by wearing a 'pro-police flag mask' in photos released by the NBA," *Daily Mail,* July 17, 2020, https://www.dailymail.com.

[63] Aila Slisco, "White Jesus Statues Should Be Torn Down, Activist Shaun King Says," *Newsweek,* June 22, 2020, https://www.newsweek.com/white-jesus-statues-should-torn-down-black-lives-matters-leader-says-1512674.

a relativism that promotes subjective feelings over objective facts.
6. Control the mainstream media (the next chapter will address how 90 percent is owned and controlled by only six companies).
7. Exert authority over social influencers, so younger generations are pressured to embrace the movement.
8. Discredit traditional American history and culture. Build mistrust and a forsaking of past leaders that encourages the tearing down of statues.
9. Present alternative, non-traditional lifestyles as normative (discussed in Chapter 1).
10. Replace traditional values with both science and mysticism; paint conventional religion as hate-based and oppression-inducing.
11. Infiltrate the church and replace the biblical gospel with a social gospel (will be discussed in Chapter 5).
12. Eliminate prayer and bar Christians from the public discourse.
13. Dismiss the American constitution as archaic and obsolete.
14. Replace the church (will also be discussed in Chapter 5).
15. Promote the BLM movement as the only qualified voice and filter through which everything must first gain approval (will also be discussed in Chapter 5).

Chapter 4
Hidden Fact Agenda

Perhaps America's biggest liar, co-founder Alicia Garza knows how to manipulate the truth. In a 2015 interview, she stated that "'black folks are being killed every 28 hours by police or vigilantes.'"[64] What do the facts show? Remember, she said "police or vigilantes." According to the FBI's Uniform Crime Reports, 90.1 percent of black victims of homicide were killed by other blacks.[65] So now the picture changes; almost all of the killings are not from the police at all, but vigilantes, from which she hopes the connotation of white supremacists will be drawn. Twisting the statistics, Garza attempts to make it seem as though police are murdering blacks almost daily. Knowing these "vigilantes" are black, why did the Black Lives Matter movement not hold a single march to protest the 90 percent of murders perpetrated against fellow blacks—why are there no speeches denouncing those in the black community who are killing our own race? How does this communicate that all

---

[64] Sunnivie Brydum, "Alicia Garza: Taking Black Lives Matter to Another Dimension," *Advocate*, December 9, 2015, https://www.advocate.com/40-under-40/2015/12/09/alicia-garza-taking-black-lives-matter-another-dimension.

[65] "Crime in the United States," *FBI- UCR*, https://ucr.fbi.gov/crime-in-the-u.s/2013/crime-in-the-u.s.-2013/offenses-known-to-law-enforcement/expanded-homicide/expanded_homicide_data_table_6_murder_race_and_sex_of_vicitm_by_race_and_sex_of_offender_2013.xls.

black lives truly matter? Does a black life only matter if it was taken at the hands of a non-black person? "Black lives matter" is an inherently moral statement, and their selectivity over black lives is grossly immoral. Each life lost represents a lost mother, father, son, daughter, brother, or sister.

    Again, 90.1 percent of black murder victims had a black killer.[66] Similarly, 83.5 percent of whites were killed by whites.[67] This is largely due to most victims of murder personally knowing their perpetrators. Interestingly, even though this trend is paralleled in racial categories, nothing is said about "white-on-white" murders. Also, the Bureau of Justice Statistics' arrest data analysis tool demonstrates that less than 1 percent of blacks overall commit a violent crime in any given year; yet the media portrays black folks as animals.[68] Ultimately, BLM strategically picks and chooses whose murder they want to protest. The movement bases its march around police brutality, but this is simply *not true*. They have also marched in protest on behalf of several transgender men whose deaths had nothing to do with police brutality. The only way to reconcile such conflicting standards is to realize that they are purposely crafting a narrative to fit

---

[66] "Crime," *FBI-UCR*.
[67] Michael Harriot, "Why We Never Talk About Black-on-Black Crime: An Answer to White America's Most Pressing Question," *The Root*, October 3, 2017, https://www.theroot.com/why-we-never-talk-about-black-on-black-crime-an-answer-1819092337.
[68] "Arrest Data Analysis Tool," *Bureau of Justice Statistics*, https://www.bjs.gov/index.cfm?ty=datool&surl=/arrests/index.cfm.

their own agenda, and it has nothing to do with black lives. Garza's cited statistic is erroneous, coming from an internal study of a fellow activist group and was quickly debunked.[69] Both left-leaning *The Guardian* and *The Washington Post* have other studies that calculated different rates than 28 hours. The FBI's crime report data does not even specify which victims were armed or unarmed, but only categorized as questionable circumstances, which does not necessarily prove any action taken by police was unjustified.[70]

Another claim is Transgender murders have been reported as "rampant," even though only 27 died in the entire year of 2019 in the country.[71] Most were not even declared a hate crime. With 1.3 million Americans identifying as "transgender," this means their risk of murder is at 0.002 percent.[72] On the other hand, 106 policemen killed out of 800,000 nationwide yields a 0.012 percent—six times

---

[69] Chava Gourarie, "Over 700 people killed by police this year. But who's counting?" *Columbia Journalism Review*, October 12, 2015, https://www.cjr.org/analysis/counting_how_many_people_are_killed_by_police_requires_more_than_arithmetic.php.

[70] Ibid.

[71] Elinor Aspegren, "Transgender murders are 'rampant' in 2020: Human Rights Campaign count 21 so far, nearly matching total of a year ago," *USA Today*, July 8, 2020, https://www.usatoday.com/story/news/nation/2020/07/08/trangender-murders-2020-human-rights-campaign/5395092002/.

[72] Tijen Butler, "What percentage of the US population is transgender?" *PinkNews*, April 2, 2019, https://www.pinknews.co.uk/2019/04/02/percentage-us-population-transgender-statistics/.

higher.[73] If transgender murders are deemed "rampant," how are officer deaths not considered a national epidemic? Not a single transgender killing was at the hands of a police officer, so why do media personalities like CNN's Don Lemon insist the movement is against police brutality when they march for transgender lives?[74]

With around 47 million blacks in the United States, 13 were killed by police officers in 2019—558 total police shootings in the same year (in a country of over 325 million), with only 111 of them black. So of the small number shot, 447 (or 80 percent) were not even black! This doesn't add up, and yet the media treats it as the most important crisis in the black community.[75] Now I am black, and I don't believe that *anyone* should be murdered, but why are we so angry about 13 deaths in the whole year when there were 18 black homicides in a single day in Chicago?[76] 64 were shot over a single weekend in

---

[73] "FBI Releases 2019 Statistics on Law Enforcement Officers Killed in the Line of Duty," *Federal Bureau of Investigation,* May 4, 2020, https://www.fbi.gov/news/pressrel/press-releases/fbi-releases-2019-statistics-on-law-enforcement-officers-killed-in-the-line-of-duty.

[74] Brian Flood, "CNN's Don Lemon scolds Terry Crews, says Black Lives Matter is about police brutality, not Black-on-Black violence," *FoxNews*, July 7, 2020, https://www.foxnews.com/media/don-lemon-terry-crews-black-lives-matter.

[75] "People shot to death by U.S. police, by race 2017-2020," Statista Research Department*, Statista,* August 6, 2020, https://www.statista.com/statistics/585152/people-shot-to-death-by-us-police-by-race/.

[76] "Report: Chicago sees its deadliest day in 60 years with 18 murders in 24 hours," *FOX6 News*, June 9, 2020, https://www.fox6now.com/news/report-chicago-sees-its-deadliest-day-in-60-years-with-18-murders-in-24-hours.

July of 2020, yet these statistics have barely been mentioned in the news over the years.[77] So what dictates the importance of a black life? Moreover, the organization claiming to defend black lives is equally silent. Again, no loss of life is ever insignificant, but such a complacent acceptance of wholesale slaughter in the streets of Chicago reveals how BLM selects only the narratives that help further their own plans. If someone truly cares about black lives, these lives matter too.

And if BLM truly cares about black lives, why not address the top killer of black lives in the America—abortion? Today, over 1 in 4 black babies are killed in the womb, a staggering statistic. This is an existential crisis; this is genocide.[78] It kills more blacks than all homicide, HIV, diabetes, accidents, cancer, and heart disease *combined*; even though black women comprise 13.3 percent of the population, they have 36 percent of all abortions.[79] In New York more back babies are aborted than born. So, does black life only matter when you deem it important?

With all of this considered, it's clear that police brutality is not actually at the heart of BLM, nor is truly caring about black lives. All of the people donating money to this

---

[77] Bryan Brammer, "64 shot, 13 killed in Chicago over weekend," *Disrn*, July 13, 2020, https://disrn.com/news/64-people-shot-13-fatally-in-chicago-over-the-weekend.

[78] "Genocide: Black Abortions in America," *Grand Rapids Right to Life*, https://www.grrtl.org/genocide/.

[79] Ibid.

organization must realize that they are not actually fighting the real threats to black life; they are using that money for their own agendas. Misleading and distorted data has certainly been a tool in BLM's arsenal. Most of their "facts" fail to be corroborated by credible research, which seriously undermines their validity. They are merely using race as a means to push their real agendas. They have discovered race is the perfect defense shield set up as a perimeter all around their organization—if a white man questions them, he is accused of racism; if a black man questions them, he is accused of treachery, like the storm of criticism that followed actor Terry Crews' comments on BLM.[80]

Black Lives Matter is not about police brutality. It's not even about equality, but a covert LGBTQ+, demonic, Marxist agenda. Why is this not widely known? The political left in America control mainstream media; they first used the term "Fake News" as a way of discrediting the countless non-traditional news outlets that have been popping up nationally to circumvent the mainstream news and get the truth out to the public. These alternative news sources are exposing the real "Fake News" that the political left want Americans to accept.

---

[80] Janelle Griffeth, "Terry Crews slammed for suggesting Black Lives Matter could morph into 'Black Lives Better,'" *NBC News*, June 30, 2020, https://www.nbcnews.com/pop-culture/celebrity/terry-crews-slammed-suggesting-black-lives-matter-could-morph-black-n1232549.

Diving deeper, I learned that there were fifty different media companies in 1983 that provided Americans with information.[81] Since 2011, just six companies now control over 90% of total media; basically, just over 200 media executives control the information provided to over 300 million Americans.[82] Those same "Big Six" own over 1500 radio stations, the biggest newspapers on three continents, and 75% of all television.[83] This does not include social media, but influencers receive their news from these sources, so they, unwittingly or otherwise, reinforce the same media narratives.

Top journalists and editors in even these liberal newsrooms are being forced to resign because they don't run to the most extreme end of the political spectrum. Lee Fang, a left-leaning reporter, for example, was accused of racism by his own colleagues for "sharing an interview with an African American man who asked, 'Why does a black life only matter when a white man takes it?'"[84] Even though he wasn't even the person who posed the question, Fang was still forced to issue a public apology or risk losing his job.[85]

---

[81] Ashley Lutz, "These 6 Corporations Control 90% of the Media in America," *Business Insider*, June 14, 2012, https://www.businessinsider.com/these-6-corporations-control-90-of-the-media-in-america-2012-6.
[82] Lutz, "Six Corporations."
[83] Ibid.
[84] Megan Basham, "When cancel culture comes to newsrooms," *WORLD Magazine*, June 22, 2020, https://world.wng.org/2020/06/when_cancel_culture_comes_to_newsrooms.
[85] Ibid.

Most of these large corporations have donated millions to BLM, so they will continue to protect their investment.[86] So if one of the "Big Six" donates millions to BLM, what incentive would they have to expose them, as it would ruin their investment? So, as much of their agenda is concealed, BLM also pursues hiding the truth.

---

[86] Aric Jenkins, "Disney makes $5 million pledge to social justice organizations," *Fortune*, June 4, 2020, https://fortune.com/2020/06/04/disney-pledge-social-justice-organizations-george-floyd/.

Chapter 5
The Church

In this chapter, I will address three major points:
1) How Black Lives Matter has deceived blacks, as well as all minorities, including the LGBTQ+ community,
2) How the organization is crafting its own "church" with a different religion, and
3) How the church should react to these truths that have been uncovered.

I could easily lay bare their desire to destroy the Christian church, simply by pointing to their leaders calling for the destruction of statues of Jesus Christ across the United States,[87] or burning Bibles en masse.[88] These actions would be more than sufficient, but once again, we will dive deeper. Throughout the first four chapters, actual motivations underlying the BLM movement have been exposed, revealing that they are not truly concerned for black lives. I have demonstrated how the movement is led by demonic forces

---

[87] Caleb Parke, "Christian Figures, symbols targeted amid ongoing protests," *Fox News*, June 25, 2020, https://www.foxnews.com/us/christian-figures-symbols-targeted-amid-black-lives-matter-protests.

[88] Adam Ford, "Video: Black Lives Matter protesters burn Bibles in Portland," *Disrn*, August 1, 2020, https://disrn.com/news/protesters-burn-bibles-in-portland.

and witchcraft, and how they can manipulate the narrative in the media to suit their own schemes.

As a black man, I was personally angered that the leadership of BLM would use the struggles of the 400 years of slavery and hardship of our community to push other agendas not even *related* to the police brutality movement. Millions of blacks, other minorities, and women are being deceived into thinking this movement is about protesting police brutality and advocating racial equality, but race has absolutely nothing to do with it. Even the LGBTQ+ community is being used within the movement's hidden agendas.

Recall that this movement thrives off of emotional reactions. They admit their "healing practice confronts the emotional, intellectual, and spiritual wounds that they and their opponents carry."[89] So the way they feel, think, and discern spiritually are all emotionally driven, and they seek to capitalize off of this in others. They know that when the black community learns of hate crimes against their race, especially from those in positions of authority, it certainly creates a visceral reaction, especially as the media's coverage purposely seeks to stoke racial tensions. And those strong reactions can, in turn, influence our mental and spiritual response.

Social injustice, for example, harms individuals, and protestors may all have that in common—they have each

---

[89] Edwards, "'Let's Imagine Something Different.'"

experienced individual hurt through racism, sexism, or other forms of discrimination. So, they are driven by that emotional hurt, and although that hurt can be incredibly real, people tend to put away logic and reason altogether as a result. Many scientific studies have proven this human tendency. Emotions can even play a dominant role in our behavior:

> Emotions influence our attitudes and judgments, which in turn, influence the decisions we make. Your success and progress largely depend on your ability to understand and interpret how you feel before making any snap judgment. Intense sadness could prevent you from taking action. Or, fear of rejection may stop you from stepping outside of your comfort zone. When you are happy the choices you make could be different from the decisions you make when you are indifferent or sad. Fear, hope, confidence and many other feelings have a substantial impact on the way we make financial decisions. Studies also show that intense emotions impair self-control. Anger and embarrassment may make you particularly vulnerable to high-risk, low payoff choices. [90]

---

[90] Thomas Oppong, "Psychologists Explain How Emotions, Not logic, Drive Human Behaviour," *Medium*, January 3, 2020, https://medium.com/personal-growth/psychologists-explain-how-emotions-not-logic-drive-human-behaviour-6ed0daf76e1a.

In summary, the problem with emotionally-driven behavior is that it will weaken our reasoning ability, and we will fail to make decisions that are in our best interest and the interests of others.

Paul warned in 2 Timothy 4:3, "For the time is coming when people will not endure sound teaching, but having itching ears they will accumulate for themselves teachers to suit their own passions." I never understood why a person would not want to hear sound teaching or the truth, because they let their emotions completely take over. So they throw sound teaching out the window; this movement is built off of emotions: "He who trusts in his own heart is a fool, / But he who walks wisely will be delivered."[91]

While the Apostle was specifically cautioning Timothy against false teachers who will deceive in order to pander to the fleshly desires of congregants, the text supports the idea that people will hear what they want to hear, even when irrational. Like a false teacher, BLM exploits the deep hurt in individuals by controlling the narrative of fake news to add fuel to the fire—this gives them power that they can use to direct followers any way they wish.

Scripture confirms that since the fall of the human race in Genesis 3, our very nature is stained and marred by the effects of the fall, including our ability to think and emote properly. In fact, God points out that our distorted hearts are

---
[91] Proverbs 28:26 (New American Standard Bible).

"deceitful above all things" and "desperately sick."[92] He then points out that even though we cannot even understand ourselves, He, in His ominiscience, searches the heart and knows us better than we do. Even when our souls are redeemed by the person and work of Christ, this deficiency still remains, but believers are given the mind of Christ through the Word and the power of the Spirit to overcome it by behaving, thinking, and emoting in a manner that is pleasing to God according to His Word.

BLM's entire political philosophy is about obtaining power, and this is their spiritual idea of "healing practice." While supporters think they have an advocate in reconciling these past hurts, the movement is actually just manipulating them to create followers to implement their hidden agendas. BLM, articulated by founder Patrisse Cullors, believes,

> This work is already taking place, but can be enhanced by spiritual resources. Spiritual power helps people claim more than a minimal existence, it orients them to a life of fulfillment. An architecture influenced by the spirituality of African-American communities is not about trying to give buildings "a soul," it is about stirring the soul in its people, building their own power,

---

[92] Jeremiah 17:9-10 (English Standard Version).

and cultivating "the audacity to imagine something different for[93] [themselves]." [94]

God says through Paul that we "do not wrestle against flesh and blood, but against the rulers, against the authorities, against the cosmic powers over this present darkness, against the spiritual forces of evil in the heavenly places."[95] The Ifà practitioner embodies the very definition of these wicked, cosmic powers who are opposed to God. Sadly, the BLM leaders worship the epitome of this scripture. The King James' Bible translates "high places," and in terms of power, heading up the Black Lives Matter organization is one of the most powerful positions on earth at this moment.

An important goal of the movement's efforts is for "social transformation [that] can have a wider effect than what we typically credit to spirituality and religion."[96] Author Elise M. Edwards observes that for the BLM founders, "spirituality cultivates an inner life."[97] The "inner life" that their primary religion of Ifà teaches is demonic possession. According to their false religion, their god Olodumare sends an Orisha spirit to possess people during a ceremonially-induced trance, imparting the ability to produce "ase," a new

---

[93] Tippett, Interview with Patrisse Cullors and Bob Ross."
[94] Edwards, "'Let's Imagine Something Different.'"
[95] Ephesians 6:12 (ESV).
[96] Edwards, "'Let's Imagine Something Different.'"
[97] Ibid.

created life.[98] Edwards summarizes, "In these movements, contemporary social justice advocates see their work as having not only political or educational aims but also emotional and spiritual intentions."[99]

Secondly, as mentioned in the beginning of the chapter, the movement is actively turning people away from the church while attempting to replace it with their own religion. BLM openly does not support the church and compels others to march in lockstep. Again, Edwards explains:

> Garza does not rely on a Christian theological framework to support her view of liberation. As Cullors has explained in her description of healing justice work, many activists in the movement were rejected in Christian churches. Black Lives Matter is queer-affirming in its participation and leadership, and although there are queer liberation Christian theologies, the dominant Christian tradition has supported heterosexual, male leadership, . . . "while our sisters, queer and trans and disabled folk take up roles in the background or not at all," Garza explains. "Any religious system that knowingly perpetuates systems of exclusion as it works toward liberation is

---

[98] "Ase," *Wikipedia,* accessed on August 12, 2020, https://en.wikipedia.org/wiki/A%E1%B9%A3%E1%BA%B9.
[99] Edwards, "'Let's Imagine Something Different.'"

incompatible with the principles undergirding Black Lives Matter."[100]

The church certainly falls under this definition of "religious system," so even they admit that Christianity and the church are fundamentally incompatible with their organization and the principles that drive it. In fact, this would include any religion system that does not embrace same sex marriage, witchcraft, Marxism, and liberation theology among other tenets, which is almost any religious institution.

Remember the platform and handbook for the Movement for Black Lives, the coalition of activist organizations with BLM in the fore, states: "We reject false solutions and believe we can achieve a complete transformation of the current systems. We also demand a defunding of the systems and institutions that criminalize and cage us."[101] To them, Christ is a false solution. Their outright denunciation of *current* systems" that "cage" them and their radical call for the total toppling of these institutions is greatly alarming. Consider how they perceive anything that prevents their mission from growing would oppress, or "cage" them. And what is that mission again? To destroy the "nuclear family structure" that God instituted and which comprises the

---

[100] Edwards, "'Let's Imagine Something Different.'"
[101] "A Vision For Black Lives," The Movement for Black Lives.

traditional American household;[102] to create a society where homosexuality and transexuality is normative; to reverse and strip away the "privileges" I possess as a heterosexual male; and to replace traditional spiritual institutions and foundations with witchcraft and voodoo. Ironically, all of these goals will "cage" us.

It is crystal clear that according to their views, the church represents a threat to their entire system of beliefs, and they have also made it abundantly clear that they will dismantle, deconstruct, defund, and destroy any system that poses such a threat. They have already asserted their influence by attempting to prevent churchgoers from entering their house of worship, then verbally and physically assaulting them.[103]

Recently, the Supreme Court ruled in favor of the LGBTQ+ community regarding sex discrimination in the workplace.[104] Citing Title VII of the Civil Rights Act of 1964, plaintiffs in three different court cases claimed that they were discriminated against by their employers because of their sexual orientation and/or gender identity. In 1964, this law

---

[102] What We Believe," *Black Lives Matter.*
[103] Steve Jordahl, "BLM fights, curses, screams, outside church service," *One News Now*, July 9, 2020, https://onenewsnow.com/church/2020/07/09/blm-fights-curses-screams-outside-church-service.
[104] Joe Carter, "Supreme Court: Employment Law Protects Sexual Orientation and Gender Identity," *The Gospel Coalition*, June 15, 2020, https://www.thegospelcoalition.org/article/court-employment-sexual-orientation-and-gender-identity/.

referred to "sex" as a person's biological gender, as it would have for the entire history of mankind. However, with this ruling, the Court interpreted "sex" to include the gender of their sexual preference and the gender they may subjectively identify as, regardless of whether it aligns with their biological makeup.[105]

This ruling affects how conservative and Christian businesses and organizations operate. For example, if a man is hired by a Catholic school to teach and coach, and then he decides to marry another man, the school is forced by law to keep him on staff, even if he has violated the church's official teachings and breached the belief statement he signed and agreed to upon hiring. The school will have no recourse and can now be sued if they decide to follow their consciences and operate the organization based on the very beliefs for which it was founded. What makes a Catholic school *Catholic* if it cannot operate according to Catholicism? And this example was not hypothetical.[106] As a Christian black man, what about my rights? Aren't all of these marches about my life mattering?

Black Lives Matter actively seeks for and recruits people who have been hurt by traditional churches.

---

[105] Carter, "Supreme Court."
[106] Tim Fitzsimons, "Fired lesbian guidance counselor sues Indianapolis archdiocese," *NBC News*, October 23, 2019, https://www.nbcnews.com/feature/nbc-out/fired-lesbian-guidance-counselor-sues-indianapolis-archdiocese-n1070681.

Remember, they are strongly against the church because it is incompatible with their organization's beliefs, and their ears are closed to hearing sound doctrine and reason, as their movement is fueled by emotional response. BLM will certainly continue to use their current power to compel the government to control the pulpit. Soon, the content of preaching, an area that exists protected by God and by the Constitution, will be regulated. Any Biblical teaching that smacks of discrimination will be targeted as "hate speech." Ultimately, this movement is aiming to weaken and destroy the church.

They have already allied themselves with LGBTQ+ activists and created a rainbow colored flag with a fist in the middle.[107] They are trying to make black rights and gay rights appear indistinguishable and one in the same, which is **not** true. God's Word is patently clear that practicing homosexuality is a grievous sin to the Creator because it rebels against His most fundamental creation of male and female, both in His image, intended for one another in the ordained union of a family. Both the Old and New Testaments condemn the practice of homosexuality.[108]

---

[107] https://www.amazon.com/Blm-Pride-Rainbow-Sticker-Waterproof/dp/B089QWTMW3.
[108] Leviticus 18:22; 20:13; Romans 1:18-32; 1 Corinthians 6:9-11; 1 Timothy 1:8-10.

According to God (whose authority would settle it alone), biological science, and basic common sense and logic, there are two genders. Humanity has known this for the entirety of its existence. Yet somehow, there are now 58 genders, according to Facebook.[109] In fact, California state law allows for fines and possible jail time for anyone caught using the incorrect preferred-gender pronoun of another.[110] With 58 genders and counting, there's a good chance people will get it wrong. There is absolutely no scientific basis for any of these man-made claims—am I even allowed to use the term "man-made" according to California law?

Self-autonomy, rather than dependence on God, is at the heart of man's sinful rebellion against His rightful reign in our lives. Yet society encourages people to determine their own identity, fundamentally rejecting the very essence of who God made them to be. But self-identification is as wishy-washy and subjective as our hearts, and certainly does not always line up with reality. What if a married partner claimed she identifies as a nine-year-old; can she press charges of pedophilia against her spouse? Could a white man identifying as black escape the label of racist when using offensive black

---

[109] Russell Goldman, "Here's a List of 58 Gender Options for Facebook Users," *ABC News*, February 13, 2014, https://abcnews.go.com/blogs/headlines/2014/02/heres-a-list-of-58-gender-options-for-facebook-users.

[110] Brooke Singman, "New California law allows jail time for using wrong gender pronoun, sponsor denies that would happen," *FoxNews*, October 9, 2017, https://www.foxnews.com/politics/new-california-law-allows-jail-time-for-using-wrong-gender-pronoun-sponsor-denies-that-would-happen.

language? The left would label such behavior as blackfishing, but why is his reality not being accepted? The left would contradict itself, revealing the lack of any shred of basic logic when objective reality gets tossed aside. If we can go to jail for mistakenly addressing someone by the wrong preferred pronoun out of 58 options, it will not be long before preaching that God created two genders will be equally illegal.

Make no mistake that they intend to replace the church with their own places of worship. According to the Associated Press, a new group called Supermajority was launched last year to "harness the political power of women:"[111]

> Three of the nation's most influential activists are launching an organization that aims to harness the political power of women to influence elections and shape local and national policy priorities. Dubbed Supermajority, the organization is the creation of Cecile Richards, the former head of Planned Parenthood; Alicia Garza, co-founder of Black Lives Matter; and Ai-jen Poo, executive director of the National Domestic Workers Alliance. The group, which describes itself as multiracial and intergenerational, has a goal of training and mobilizing 2 million women

---

[111] Julie Pace, "New group launches to harness political power of women," *Associated Press,* April 28, 2019, https://apnews.com/a60b6733819c4e399f0051eaf73ea276.

over the next year to become organizers and political leaders in their communities.¹¹²

The political agenda pushed by this organization is steeped in value judgments that are based on *their* ethical standards, so these leaders will be shaping the moral fabric of a community as well, all informed by their queer-affirming, Marxist-radicalizing, witchcraft-practicing, abortion-defending views. And they will be training these leaders to recruit more followers for their cause.

They claim that their goal is to assemble in the community, a replacement for the role of the church. The Bible calls believers to "consider one another to provoke unto love and to good works: Not forsaking the assembling of ourselves together, as the manner of some is; but exhorting one another: and so much the more, as ye see the day approaching."¹¹³ So, the church "assembles" to build up one another and encourage good works; this is a primary role within the local church, and this movement's usurpation of this role will ultimately end in the opposite as they focus on tearing down.

Employing women is purposefully done, in order to engender that emotional response they seek to evoke, as God has specially and specifically created each gender with certain

---
¹¹² Pace, "New group launches."
¹¹³ Hebrews 10:24-25 (King James Version).

proclivities; among those tendencies, women on the whole are prone to be more affected by emotion. The movement seeks to harness this, as afore-mentioned in the use of manipulating emotion to keep people from rationally evaluating their claims. They are also using a façade of "liberation" to make it appear that women were not equal before. This propensity to sensitivity in women is actually a beautiful blessing from God, as this helps them in nurturing their children with kindness and compassion and creating a loving, caring home in which the family can thrive. However, as with any gift God gives to mankind, sinful hearts can pervert and distort this blessing to use it for evil intent. In fact, these emotions can rapidly become dangerous when informed by fallacies. Women also possess incredible power to influence men, for good or for ill. The Bible provides numerous examples of both, condemning the wicked use and praising the proper use: "A wife with strength of character is the crown of her husband."[114]

Tearing down the church is not just a goal for BLM, but it's the actual main purpose. We have reviewed all of the ulterior motives in the last few chapters, and they have built up this last, final aim. Even after reading all of the evidence in this book, some professing Christians will *still* support the movement—the pressure is just too strong. There are several types of responses:
    1) Those who don't agree with everything in the movement, such as the witchcraft, but still want to

---
[114] Proverbs 12:4 (God's Word Translation).

support social justice because of the rampant *in*justice,
2) Those who don't want to support BLM anymore, but see no viable alternative for Christians,
3) Those who disagree with BLM because of everything explained thus far, but are just too scared to speak out against it, for fear of being labeled a racist if white, and a traitor if black, and
4) Those who read the book, but don't care because they don't participate in BLM anyway, so they see no reason for spreading this truth.

Addressing the last group first, Christians *must* care because Christ calls us to care. He tells us to proclaim the truth, and we expose spiritual lies, especially when they infiltrate the church. God calls us to be aware of wolves in sheep's clothing. While the Apostle was referring to false teachers in the church, the same principle applies because of the spiritual nature of their movement. The Bible declares that the "the fruit of light is found in all that is good and right and true," and exhorts us to "try to discern what is pleasing to the Lord," and to "[t]ake no part in the unfruitful works of darkness, but instead expose them."[115] This means believers should not associate with the Black Lives Matter organization, and should even labor to expose the truth of their real intentions. It does **not** mean we cannot fight for social injustice (racism is a grievous sin to the Lord), nor does it

---
[115] Ephesians 5:9-11 (ESV).

mean we cannot confront systemic racism, but it ***does*** mean ***NO*** support for BLM.

Now, some pastors may point out other major social issues—drugs, the rise of foster care, human trafficking, crime and suicide rates—and disregard unveiling BLM as a top priority. But this would be ***wrong***. This is actually the most important social issue right now for four reasons:
1) No other issue is a movement where anyone who does not actively support them is immediately considered a violent enemy,
2) No other movement is fracturing the church by dividing people over race, and seeking to destroy the church (such as when they burn Bibles at protests),
3) No other movement is attacking a pastor's flock, while pastors are serving up soft sermons of self-help and the prosperity gospel; soon, their pulpits and mics will be stripped away as religious liberties are under attack by the government, spurred on by this organization, and
4) No other movement is spreading misinformation, upending social norms, and aiming to destroy every institution that undermines its goals.

Though these other social issues should certainly catch our attention, pastors can address them from the pulpit; however, if this movement is not addressed now, there likely won't be a pulpit left from which to preach.

Next, the Black Lives Matter organization does not represent the righteous movement as a whole; it's the official name of an incorporated foundation. If you are protesting Apple, for example, it does not mean you are against phones and technology in general; it means you oppose that specific company. When BLM is mentioned (especially in capital letters), this is in reference to the official organization and its movement, not the larger, general movement that promotes the principle that black lives truly do matter: I support white people, but that does not mean I will march with the KKK. There is a difference, and that difference with Black Lives Matter has become confusing and muddled. In fact, BLM cleverly picked such a name as a built-in protection for them to silence their adversaries—who would dare say they oppose an organization called Black Lives Matter? *Only a racist*, they hope people will think.

Again, some believers may say that they only partially agree with BLM's views; they may support equality, but reject the rest of the agenda. However, the conduct and decisions of believers' must be dictated by the principles in God's Word. God has much to say on this topic, and there is no middle ground. God intensely warns His children of the dangers of flirting with wicked people:

> I do not sit with men of falsehood,
>   nor do I consort with hypocrites.

> I hate the assembly of evildoers,
>   and I will not sit with the wicked.[116]

> Blessed is the man
>   who walks not in the counsel of the wicked,
> nor stands in the way of sinners,
>   nor sits in the seat of scoffers;[117]

> You shall not fall in with the many to do evil, nor shall you bear witness in a lawsuit, siding with the many, so as to pervert justice.[118]

> Do not be deceived: "Bad company ruins good morals."[119]

I met a Christian once who was marching for equality, and holding up a sign that read "Black Trans Life Matters"—why? Because he was down for the movement. But again, there is no middle ground. What if I partially agree with the Bible? Or do I become partially saved, with only part of me going to heaven? Christians cannot simply pick and choose what parts of BLM they want to align themselves with; there is no Biblical principle from scripture to support that. If believers claim that Christ is the head of their lives, they must

---

[116] Psalm 26:4-5 (ESV).
[117] Psalm 1:1 (ESV).
[118] Exodus 23:2.
[119] 1 Corinthians 15:33.

obey His word. Christ says that doing that very thing is how we will know if we are truly in Him: "'If you love me, you will keep my commandments.'"[120]

In fact, God has a very direct principle from scripture regarding believers and unbelievers engaging in a spiritual endeavor together. The Apostle Paul states:

> Do not be unequally yoked with unbelievers. For what partnership has righteousness with lawlessness? Or what fellowship has light with darkness? What accord has Christ with Belial? Or what portion does a believer share with an unbeliever? What agreement has the temple of God with idols? For we are the temple of the living God;[121]

Many take these verses out of context as a reason to not even interact with unbelievers in life, but that interpretation is incorrect, as scripture bears out that we are called to be *in* the world to evangelize and shine the light of Christ's love in the saving message of the gospel, but not to be *of* the world by living life according to the flesh. Instead, Paul is referring to spiritual endeavors, of which one of the most important is marriage. The bonds of matrimony are inherently spiritual, and so an application of this principle is for a believer to not wed an unbeliever. In the same way, we have clearly

---
[120] John 14:15.
[121] 2 Corinthians 6:14-16.

demonstrated that BLM is a self-confessed, spiritual movement and their spiritual beliefs are evil, ungodly, and of Satanic origin. Involvement with their organization, then, is forbidden, as their Ifà-driven values are incompatible with God's clear command. This command is graciously given to protect us and protect His Name.

Finally, some Christians feel that if they don't march with them, they are neglecting the duty to fight injustice. I actually hear this argument frequently. But remember, the official Black Lives Matter organization is a corporation—it's not the whole movement; it's its *own* movement. Just because you don't support their organization does not mean you are against equality. The fight for equality and Black Lives Matter Global Network Foundation are two separate entities. Wake up, church folks. Slavery is not new—remember Egypt? Satan loves division in the church that foments hate. The Bible contains "all things that pertain to life and godliness" and is fully sufficient to counsel us in this relevant matter.[122] When the Bible speaks, God speaks, and we don't need a manmade slogan to hold up after that. He has graciously given us sixty-six books from over forty men spanning 1500 years to fight social injustice properly and in a manner that pleases and glorifies Him.

Christians profess that God is all-powerful and always ruling on His throne—that He can change anyone and direct

---

[122] 2 Peter 1:3 (NASB).

everything underneath His Sovereign reign, and then when Memorial Day 2020 struck in Minneapolis, we tossed our Bibles to the ground and picked up a manmade sign endorsing a demonic organization and held it up high, professing the name of George Floyd instead of Jesus Christ. Videos show people chanting, "Black Lives Matter!" and "George Floyd," while bowing their knees. But scripture says that "at the name of Jesus every knee should bow, in heaven and on earth and under the earth, and every tongue confess that Jesus Christ is Lord, to the glory of God the Father."[123] So, why do we kneel to them and not unto God?

People are complaining that the church is doing nothing, but we must remember that the church is the people, not the building. That means if you are a believer, ***you*** are the church! You are grumbling against yourselves! Let's be real—you are doing nothing through Christ against this social injustice, so stop saying the church isn't doing anything! Perhaps just honestly admit that you don't read your Bible and don't know what to do. But the good news is that the Bible has the answers you seek. Quit starving yourself, believer! Feed on the Word. The Bible is how God has chosen to communicate to us who He is, who we really are, what He's done for us, and what He expects from us: We are all sinners; Christ died for sinners; we repent and believe in Christ and His provision as the substitutionary Lamb, and now we are called by God to live like Christ! He doesn't just expect us to figure it out—He

---
[123] Philippians 2:10-11 (ESV).

has shared everything we need to "walk in a manner worthy of the calling to which [we] have been called."[124]

Jesus commands: "But I say unto you, Love your enemies, bless them that curse you, do good to them that hate you, and pray for them which despitefully use you, and persecute you."[125] Christ's words were already recorded for you to handle this, and we must listen. Instead of marching against police, did Christians seek to pray for them, even though they are not the enemy? Did we go and hold a cop's hand and pray for them as the Jesus told us to do? Did we pray for the officer who killed George Floyd? Did we forgive him? God tells us to "[b]e kind to one another, tenderhearted, forgiving one another, as God in Christ forgave you."[126] How can I be utterly overwhelmed at the pure grace and mercy the Creator of the Universe bestowed on me by forgiving my heinous sins against Him, and yet turn around and refuse to grant forgiveness to a fellow sinner? True forgiveness is a Christian concept. It is precisely because Christ graciously bore the wrath due to me for all my sins against Him that I am now free and able to forgive others, even of the most monstrous offenses. To say a crime is too egregious to warrant forgiveness is to say Christ's sacrifice is too weak to cover my sins.

---

[124] Ephesians 4:1 (ESV).
[125] Matthew 5:44 (KJV).
[126] Ephesians 4:32 (ESV).

I spoke to a pastor on my journey to spread this word, and I asked him what he would say if the cop that killed George Floyd had randomly called him and asked to be led to Christ. He responded that he would first tell him how the officer had done all of us wrong. I stopped him. When we asked Christ for forgiveness, did He inform us that He first needs to go over each and every thorn we put in His head? Each whip lash across His back? No! He accepted us with open arms, so why do we refuse to preach God's Word over our own strong emotional reactions? Why must our message of personal hurt come before God's mercy? Why do we attach strings when He attached none for us?

If God is our head, our life, our hope, and our love, are we willing to stand up for what we love? He commands us to speak the truth in love, and that begins with first exposing them. Secondly, God is looking for children to expose the wolves. Psalm 94:16 asks, "**Who** rises up for me against the wicked? **Who** stands up for me against evildoers?"(emphasis added) Thirdly, they should be sharply rebuked:

> For there are many who are insubordinate, empty talkers and deceivers, especially those of the circumcision party. They must be silenced, since they are upsetting whole families by teaching for shameful gain what they ought not to teach. One of the Cretans, a prophet of their own, said, "Cretans are always liars, evil beasts, lazy gluttons." This testimony is true.

Therefore rebuke them sharply, that they may be sound in the faith.[127]

The word "rebuke" means to express sharp disapproval of someone's behavior. If a Christian is marching with this demonic organization, or if a church has the BLM name emblazoned on their pulpit, they must be sharply rebuked. Why do we rebuke and expose the truth? James 5:20 says, "Let him know that whoever brings back a sinner from his wandering will save his soul from death and will cover a multitude of sins."

The last group remaining in our list of reactions to this information were those who know the truth, but will refuse to share it for fear of being labeled either racist or treacherous. It could be fear from pastors who don't want to lose members or create division, or Christians in secular professions who fear losing their jobs, or teachers who are required to teach the subject—I call you **cowardly**. In reality, earthly peace has become an idol in their lives, because Christ does not promise that it will be easy or that society will accept them—He promises the opposite: "[A]nd you will be hated by all for My Name's sake. But the one who endures to the end will be saved."[128]

---

[127] Titus 1:10-13 (ESV).
[128] Matthew 10:22 (ESV).

The Bible instructs us to speak up and stand up for God, but many professing believers are afraid of the pressure of persecution. We must remember we should fear God, not man:

> "But as for the cowardly, the faithless, the detestable, as for murderers, the sexually immoral, sorcerers, idolaters, and all liars, their portion will be in the lake that burns with fire and sulfur, which is the second death."[129]

> "For whoever is ashamed of me and of my words, of him will the Son of Man be ashamed when He comes in His glory and the glory of the Father and of the holy angels."[130]

> "... but whoever denies Me before men, I also will deny before My Father who is in heaven."[131]

> You adulterous people! Do you not know that friendship with the world is enmity with God? Therefore whoever wishes to be a friend of the world makes himself an enemy of God.[132]

---

[129] Revelation 21:8.
[130] Luke 9:26.
[131] Matthew 10:33.
[132] James 4:4 (ESV)

Do not love the world or the things in the world. If anyone loves the world, the love of the Father is not in him.[133]

---

[133] 1 John 2:15.

Final Thoughts

As a black Christian, I believe that this is not a *skin* problem—it's a *sin* problem. Proverbs 14:34 says, "Righteousness exalts a nation, but sin is a reproach to any people." The word "righteousness" in this passage is not referring to an individual's right standing with God, but to a nation that adheres to God's righteous standards as found in His moral law.

There are hidden agendas being pushed underneath the label of "race" that actually have nothing to do with race. This is spiritual warfare, and the soul has no color. The Bible makes it **very** clear who our enemy is: The fight is "not against flesh and blood" because it's a spiritual fight. So why are we fighting each other because of the color of our "flesh?"[134] Why are we getting angry over the flesh when Paul says, "For I know that in me (that is, in my flesh,) dwelleth no good thing?"[135] Why are we getting angry over the flesh when that's **not** what we should be fighting over? This is causing division in our country and especially in the church. This movement is literally going to take away the pulpit and limit what pastors can and cannot do in the church. The aim of the movement is to destroy the church, and the first step is to cause division in the body of Christ.

---

[134] Ephesians 6:12 (NASB).
[135] Romans 7:18 (KJV).

Minority believers, why do we defend our race more than God? We say God is the head of our lives, so why are we wearing #blackmen shirts when it should be #christianmen shirts? If God is the **head** of our lives and in **all** that we do, if being a child of God is our foremost identity, we need to promote Him first. Why are we holding manmade signs when God already gave us His Word to uphold?

We say we are believers following the lead of the Holy Spirit, but what happens to the Holy Spirit when someone mentions race? As I have dialogued with the black church, it is clear that *we put our race above our God*. As a Christian, we claim God's headship in our lives, but when a person proclaims hatred toward God and the things of the Lord, we seek to determine what is causing the person's hurt, but there's usually no visceral reaction to this disavowal of our Lord—the One whom we love more than anyone and anything. Yet let a white person proclaim hatred toward blacks—instant anger arises. Why does this cause a bigger reaction? Why do we defend our skin more than the One who created us and our skin? Do we forget about Christ as our example when contending with the devil as he seeks an opportunity to tempt us to unrighteous anger?

I know many will say this is extreme and they certainly do not prioritize skin before Christ, but they still react in sinful anger. If that's you, why do you let the devil tempt you to sin using the same trick of racism? Others may say they take offense to such an accusation, but "offense" is something one voluntarily chooses to take. Will you let the devil use race to derail you from our real mission here as Christians—to win souls—or will you run to Christ Jesus through whom you can be an overcomer of hatred?

In the future, the media, athletes, entertainers, and social influencers will continue to partake in boycotts, refusing to play sports, make films, etc. These activities have nothing to do with our mission as Christians. The Bible says we are in the world at this time, but we are no longer of it; this is not our home. When we all die—black, white, brown, blue, green—our souls depart to eternity, and it's our commission from Christ Himself to proclaim the Gospel, so that souls may respond and reach heaven.

Be looking out for *Expose Them 2*, which will deal with exactly how society is destroying the church in plain daylight. Focusing on Big TECH companies that literally have PLANS to censor anything Christian related, hidden agendas, as well as how SATAN is directly attacking Christians, and we do not even know it. There are movements funded by groups to literally remove the bible out of circulation, force transgender bathrooms in churches, and prevent you from preaching OUR gospel in the church. Yes, these movements have ALREADY started, already have millions of dollars and are WORKING behind the scenes. "Churches" based on witchcraft (masked under social injustice) that will be showing up over the next few years. I will continue to expose the wolf in sheep clothing.

People Parish because lack of knowledge…
Now that you read this book, you are NOW accountable!!!

How you can Help

When god called me, I walked away from a 6-figure job the SAME DAY to research and teach this message along with the messages below. I work 100% from donations. Please donate so we can continue to uncover the wolf in sheep clothing for the body of Christ.

Go to www.mckinneygroup.org   to donate.

To Invite me to talk at your church send an email to

exposethem4god@gmail.com or go to the website.

I teach on

1. Exposing hidden agendas in our mainstream society's,
2. Exposing the false doctrine being taught in the churches, stop taking ques from the world and start taking them from GOD.

3. Teach real gospel, not prosperity or "feel good "messages.
4. Teach you how to walk as the Real salt of the earth and light of the world.
5. Teach on how to operate in the spiritual gifts,
6. Bring real revival with tangible power (manifestation) BACK to the church.

Be LOOKING OUT FOR EXPOSE THEM 2

- **Learn the hidden ways society is destroying the church in plain daylight**
- **Learn how BIG TECH companies and mainstream media will censor anything Christian related and how they are raising money to remove freedom of speech in the church**
- **Learn about hidden (and not so hidden) plans by big tech and big government to remove Bibles from circulation and force churches to adopt anti-Christian policies like same-sex marriage**
- **Learn how most Christians are supporting an anti-Christian agenda without even knowing it**
- **Learn how Satan is directly attacking Christians without their knowledge!**
- **And more. Much more.**

Bibliography

Angeleti, Gabriella. "Watch Patrisse Cullors' 'Prayer to the Iyami' Performance." *The Art Newspaper*, June 4, 2020. https://www.theartnewspaper.com/video/patrisse-cullors-prayer-to-the-iyami.

Aspegren, Elinor. "Transgender murders are 'rampant' in 2020: Human Rights Campaign count 21 so far, nearly matching total of a year ago." *USA Today*, July 8, 2020. https://www.usatoday.com/story/news/nation/2020/07/08/trangender-murders-2020-human-rights-campaign/5395092002/.

Basham, Megan. "When cancel culture comes to newsrooms." *WORLD Magazine*, June 22, 2020. https://world.wng.org/2020/06/when_cancel_culture_comes_to_newsrooms.

Black Lives Matter. "What We Believe." Accessed August 12, 2020. https://blacklivesmatter.com/what-we-believe/.

Brammer, Bryan. "64 shot, 13 killed in Chicago over weekend." *Disrn*, July 13, 2020. https://disrn.com/news/64-people-shot-13-fatally-in-chicago-over-the-weekend.

Brinckmann, Suan. "Witchcraft Invades the BLM Movement." *Women of Grace*, June 16, 2020. https://www.womenofgrace.com/blog/?p=72316.

Brydum, Sunnivie. "Alicia Garza: Taking Black Lives Matter to Another

Dimension." *Advocate*, December 9, 2015.
https://www.advocate.com/40-under-40/2015/12/09/alicia-garza-taking-black-lives-matter-another-dimension.

Bureau of Justice Statistics. "Arrest Data Analysis Tool."
https://www.bjs.gov/index.cfm?ty=datool&surl=/arrests/index.cfm.

Burnley, Lawrence. "The Movement for Black Lives Has Always Been Spiritual." *Yes! Magazine,* June 19, 2020.
https://www.yesmagazine.org/opinion/2020/06/19/black-lives-movement-spiritual/.

Butler, Tijen. "What percentage of the US population is transgender?" *PinkNews,* April 2, 2019.
https://www.pinknews.co.uk/2019/04/02/percentage-us-population-transgender-statistics/.

Carter, Joe. "Supreme Court: Employment Law Protects Sexual Orientation and Gender Identity." *The Gospel Coalition*, June 15, 2020.
https://www.thegospelcoalition.org/article/court-employment-sexual-orientation-and-gender-identity/.

Court, Andrew. "'I thought it looked cool!' Houston Rockets star James Harden said he didn't intend to make a political statement after he sparked outrage by wearing a 'pro-police flag mask' in photos released by the NBA." *Daily Mail*, July 17, 2020.
https://www.dailymail.com.

Cunningham, William Michael. "Black Lives Matter: Corporate America has Pledged at least $1.678 Billion So Far." *Black Enterprise*, June 10, 2020.

        https://www.blackenterprise.com/black-lives-matter-corporate-america-has-pledged-1-678-billion-so-far/.

Davidson, John Daniel. "If You Don't Support Black Lives Matter, You're Fired." *The Federalist*, June 11, 2020. https://thefederalist.com/2020/06/11/if-you-dont-support-black-lives-matter-youre-fired/.

Dunleavy, Jerry. "Black Lives Matter fundraising handled by group with convicted terrorist on its board." *Washington Examiner*, June 25, 2020. https://www.washingtonexaminer.com/news/black-lives-matter-fundraising-handled-by-group-with-convicted-terrorist-on-its-board.

Edwards, Elise M. "'Let's Imagine Something Different': Spiritual Principles in Contemporary African American Justice Movements and Their Implications for the Built Environment." *Religions* 8, no. 12 (2017): https://www.mdpi.com/2077-1444/8/12/256/htm.

Farrag, Hebah. "The Fight for Black Lives is a Spiritual Movement." *Berkely Center for Religion, Peace, and World Affairs, Georgetown University*, June 9, 2020. https://berkleycenter.georgetown.edu/responses/the-fight-for-black-lives-is-a-spiritual-movement.

Farrag, Hebah. "The Role of the Spirit in the #blacklivesmatter Movement: A Conversation with Activist and Artist Patrisse Cullors." *Religion Dispatches*, June 24, 2015. https://religiondispatches.org/the-role-of-spirit-in-the-blacklivesmatter-movement-a-conversation-with-activist-and-artist-patrisse-cullors/.

FBI-UCR. "Crime in the United States." https://ucr.fbi.gov/crime-in-the-u.s/2013/crime-in-the-u.s.-2013/offenses-known-to-law-enforcement/expanded-homicide/expanded homicide data table 6 murder race and sex of vicitm by race and sex of offender 2013.xls.

Federal Bureau of Investigation. "FBI Releases 2019 Statistics on Law Enforcement Officers Killed in the Line of Duty," May 4, 2020. https://www.fbi.gov/news/pressrel/press-releases/fbi-releases-2019-statistics-on-law-enforcement-officers-killed-in-the-line-of-duty.

Federal Bureau of Prisons. "Orisha Worshipers." https://www.bop.gov/foia/docs/orishamanual.pdf.

Fitzsimons, Tim. "Fired lesbian guidance counselor sues Indianapolis archdiocese." *NBC News*, October 23, 2019. https://www.nbcnews.com/feature/nbc-out/fired-lesbian-guidance-counselor-sues-indianapolis-archdiocese-n1070681.

Flood, Brian. "CNN's Don Lemon scolds Terry Crews, says Black Lives Matter is about police brutality, not Black-on-Black violence." *FoxNews*, July 7, 2020, https://www.foxnews.com/media/don-lemon-terry-crews-black-lives-matter.

Ford, Adam. "Video: Black Lives Matter protesters burn Bibles in Portland." *Disrn*, August 1, 2020. https://disrn.com/news/protesters-burn-bibles-in-portland.

FOX6 News. "Report: Chicago sees its deadliest day in 60 years with 18 murders in 24 hours." June 9, 2020. https://www.fox6now.com/news/report-chicago-sees-its-deadliest-day-in-60-years-with-18-murders-in-24-hours.

Goldman, Russell. "Here's a List of 58 Gender Options for Facebook Users." *ABC News*, February 13, 2014. https://abcnews.go.com/blogs/headlines/2014/02/heres-a-list-of-58-gender-options-for-facebook-users.

Gourarie, Chava. "Over 700 people killed by police this year. But who's counting?" *Columbia Journalism Review*, October 12, 2015. https://www.cjr.org/analysis/counting_how_many_people_are_killed_by_police_requires_more_than_arithmetic.php.

Grand Rapids Right to Life. "Genocide: Black Abortions in America," https://www.grrtl.org/genocide/.

Griffeth, Janelle. "Terry Crews slammed for suggesting Black Lives Matter could morph into 'Black Lives Better.' *NBC News*, June 30, 2020. https://www.nbcnews.com/pop-culture/celebrity/terry-crews-slammed-suggesting-black-lives-matter-could-morph-black-n1232549.

Harriot, Michael. "Why We Never Talk About Black-on-Black Crime: An Answer to White America's Most Pressing Question." *The Root*, October 3, 2017. https://www.theroot.com/why-we-never-talk-about-black-on-black-crime-an-answer-1819092337.

Haynes, Allana. "The Great Divide: Why The Church Isn't Connecting With #BLM." *Religion Unplugged*, May 29, 2020. https://religionunplugged.com/news/2017/7/25/the-church-and-black-lives-matter.

Horvat II, John. "Witches and Satanists have teamed up with leftists to destroy America." *Lifesite News*, June 16, 2020. https://www.lifesitenews.com/opinion/witches-and-satanists-have-teamed-up-with-leftists-to-destroy-america.

Houston, Jennifer. "LGBTQ Organizations Stand in Solidarity with Black Lives Matter." *Neighborhood Funders Group,* December 3, 2015. https://www.nfg.org/news/lgbtq-organizations-stand-solidarity-black-lives-matter.

Ifà Religion. "Iyanifa Ifa Priestess." https://ifa-odu.com/iyanifa-ifa-priestess/.

Iyanifa. "Iyanifa, Women of Wisdom." http://www.iyanifa.org/home.html.

Jenkins, Aric Jenkins. "Disney makes $5 million pledge to social justice organizations." *Fortune*, June 4, 2020. https://fortune.com/2020/06/04/disney-pledge-social-justice-organizations-george-floyd/.

Jordahl, Steve. "BLM fights, curses, screams, outside church service." *One News Now*, July 9, 2020. https://onenewsnow.com/church/2020/07/09/blm-fights-curses-screams-outside-church-service.

Kerr, Andrew. "A Convicted Terrorist Sits On Board Of Charity Handling Black Lives Matter Fundraising." *Daily Caller*, June 27, 2020. https://dailycaller.com/2020/06/27/convicted-terrorist-black-lives-matter-thousand-currents/.

Khan-Cullors, Patrisse, and Asha Bandele. *When They Call You a Terrorist: A Black Lives Matter Memoir*. New York: St. Martin's Publishing Group, 2018.

"The Leading Global Thinkers of 2015." Advocates. *Foreign Policy*. https://2015globalthinkers.foreignpolicy.com/#!advocates/list.

Lloyd, Vincent, et al. "Religion, secularism, and Black Lives Matter." *The Immanent Frame, Social Science Research Council*, September 22, 2016.
https://tif.ssrc.org/2016/09/22/religion-secularism-and-black-lives-matter/.

Lutz, Ashley. "These 6 Corporations Control 90% of the Media in America." *Business Insider*, June 14, 2012.
https://www.businessinsider.com/these-6-corporations-control-90-of-the-media-in-america-2012-6.

Merriam-Webster Dictionary. "cisgender." "heteronormative." Accessed August 12, 2020.
www.merriam-webster.com.

Molina, Alejandra. "Black Lives Matter is 'a spiritual movement,' says co-founder Patrisse Cullors." *Religion News Service*, June 15, 2020.
https://religionnews.com/2020/06/15/why-black-lives-matter-is-a-spiritual-movement-says-blm-co-founder-patrisse-cullors/.

The Movement for Black Lives. "A Vision For Black Lives: Policy Demands for Black Power, Freedom, and Justice."
https://neweconomy.net/resources/vision-black-lives-policy-demands-black-power-freedom-and-justice.

National Criminal Justice Reference Service. "FBI Analysis of Terrorist Incidents and Terrorist Related Activities in the United States 1984."
https://www.ncjrs.gov/pdffiles1/Digitization/120257NCJRS.pdf.

Oppong, Thomas Oppong. "Psychologists Explain How Emotions, Not logic, Drive Human Behaviour." *Medium*, January 3, 2020.
https://medium.com/personal-growth/psychologists-explain-how-emotions-not-logic-drive-human-behaviour-6ed0daf76e1a.

Pace, Julie. "New group launches to harness political power of women." *Associated Press,* April 28, 2019.
https://apnews.com/a60b6733819c4e399f0051eaf73ea276.

Parke, Caleb. "Christian Figures, symbols targeted amid ongoing protests." *Fox News*, June 25, 2020.
https://www.foxnews.com/us/christian-figures-symbols-targeted-amid-black-lives-matter-protests.

Penniman, Leah. *Farming While Black: Soul Fire Farm's Practical Guide to Liberation on the Land.* White River Junction, VT: Chelsea Green Publishing, 2018.

Phillips, Morgan. "Could Black Lives Matter get on the ballot?" *Fox News,* June 25, 2020.
https://www.foxnews.com/politics/black-lives-matter-ballot.

Richardson, Valerie. "'We are trained Marxists': Black Lives Matter co-founder featured in GOP ad." *The Washington Times,* June 25, 2020.
https://www.washingtontimes.com/news/2020/jun/25/patrisse-cullors-black-lives-matter-co-founder-fea/.

Salzman, Sony. "From the start, Black Lives Matter has been about LGBTQ live." *Religion Unplugged,* June 21, 2020.
https://religionunplugged.com/news/2017/7/25/the-church-and-black-lives-matter.

Shenvi, Neil and Pat Sawyer. "The Incompatibility of Critical Theory and Christianity." *The Gospel Coalition,* May 15, 2019.
https://www.thegospelcoalition.org/article/incompatibility-critical-theory-christianity/.

Singman, Brooke. "New California law allows jail time for using wrong

gender pronoun, sponsor denies that would happen." *FoxNews,* October 9, 2017.
https://www.foxnews.com/politics/new-california-law-allows-jail-time-for-using-wrong-gender-pronoun-sponsor-denies-that-would-happen.

Slisco, Aila. "White Jesus Statues Should Be Torn Down, Activist Shaun King Says." *Newsweek,* June 22, 2020.
https://www.newsweek.com/white-jesus-statues-should-torn-down-black-lives-matters-leader-says-1512674.

Statista. "People shot to death by U.S. police, by race 2017-2020," August 6, 2020.
https://www.statista.com/statistics/585152/people-shot-to-death-by-us-police-by-race/.

Tippett, Krista. Interview with Patrissee Cullors and Bob Ross. "On Being with Krista Tippett: Patrisse Cullors + Bob Ross, The Spiritual Work of Black Lives Matter." *National Public Radio*, February 18, 2016.
https://onbeing.org/programs/patrisse-cullors-and-robert-ross-the-spiritual-work-of-black-lives-matter-may2017/.

Walters, John. "Communism Killed 94M in 20th Century, Feels Need to Kill Again." *Reason*, March 13, 2013.
https://reason.com/2013/03/13/communism-killed-94m-in-20th-century/.

Wikipedia. "Black Lives Matter." "Nuclear Family." "Ifà." "Iyalawo." "Yoruba People." "Iyami Aje." "Marxism." "Communism." "Ase." Accessed August 12, 2020.
www.wikipedia.org.

Zdanowicz, Christina and Artemis Moshtaghian. "Two people are charged with a hate crime for vandalizing a Black Lives Matter mural." *CNN*, July 7, 2020. https://www.cnn.com/2020/07/07/us/hate-crime-charges-black-lives-matter-mural-painted-over-trnd/index.html.

Picture of Ifa Worship, courtesy of Wikipedia. Accessed on August 12, 2020, https://en.wikipedia.org/wiki/Yoruba_religion#/media/File:Obatala_Priester_im_Tempel.jpg.

Picture of Book Cover for Ifa Religion, courtesy of Amazon. Accessed on August 12, 2020, https://www.amazon.com/Olodumare-Yoruba-Belief-Bolayi-Idowu/dp/1881316963.

Picture of Cullors' Performance, courtesy of The Art Newspaper. Accessed on August 12, 2020, https://www.theartnewspaper.com/video/patrisse-cullors-prayer-to-the-iyami.

Made in the USA
Columbia, SC
07 March 2021